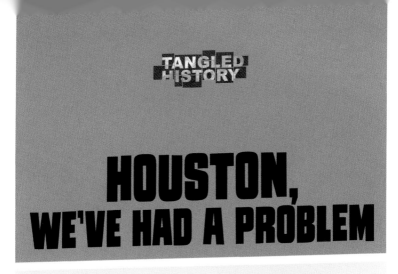

TANGLED HISTORY

HOUSTON, WE'VE HAD A PROBLEM

The Story of the Apollo 13 Disaster

BY REBECCA RISSMAN

Consultant:
Richard Bell, PhD
Associate Professor of History
University of Maryland, College Park

CAPSTONE PRESS
a capstone imprint

Tangled History is published by Capstone Press,
1710 Roe Crest Drive, North Mankato, Minnesota 56003
www.mycapstone.com

Library of Congress Cataloging-in-Publication data is available on the Library of
Congress website.

978-1-5157-7940-7 (library binding)
978-1-5157-7964-3 (paperback)
978-1-5157-7968-1 (eBook PDF)

Editorial Credits
Adrian Vigliano, editor; Bobbie Nuytten, designer; Svetlana Zhurkin, media
researcher; Katy LaVigne, production specialist

Photo Credits
Getty Images: Time Life Pictures/Bill Eppridge, 61, 92; NASA, cover, 4, 7, 8, 15, 18, 23,
30, 32, 37, 46, 57, 58, 65, 69, 70, 78, 80, 87, 97, 99, 100, 105; Newscom: Zuma Press/
Keystone Pictures USA, 53; Shutterstock: Sergey Kohl, 103; Wikimedia: Tyler
Rubach, 43

Printed and bound in the United States of America.
010780S18

TABLE OF CONTENTS

Astronaut Buzz Aldrin was the second human to set foot on the moon. He did so with the Apollo 11 mission in 1969.

FOREWORD

In 1970 watching the evening news was an American family ritual. Families would gather and listen as newscasters such as Walter Cronkite filled them in on the state of the nation. In April of that year, Cronkite could hardly cover all the updates in his 30-minute time slot. The Beatles had broken up. The war in Vietnam was raging, causing turmoil among Americans.

The women's liberation movement was sweeping the country. It inspired women to work outside the home, advocate for their own independence, and even burn their bras. And, the National Aeronautics and Space Administration (NASA) was about to send yet another crew of astronauts to the moon.

Early NASA space missions had captured the imagination and heart of the country. The first astronauts were celebrities. *Life* magazine followed them and their families, recording what they ate, the sports they enjoyed, and where they liked to travel. As *Apollo 13* prepared for launch, nearly nine years had passed since NASA had sent its first astronaut into space. Some Americans had grown bored with the space program. Many who had followed breathlessly as Neil Armstrong walked on the moon in 1969 now looked elsewhere for excitement. NASA had projected an image of perfection for years and Americans had come to believe it. They expected another successful, but uneventful, mission.

For people outside of the space industry, NASA seemed like an extremely safe organization. In reality, few things at NASA were perfect.

For instance, the Apollo spacecraft was notoriously unreliable. Just three years earlier, the crew of *Apollo 1* had burned to their deaths during a routine test in Florida. NASA technicians stood feet from the craft, unable to save the crew as flames belched from its seams. Subsequent Apollo missions had been more successful but experienced plenty of glitches of their own.

When Jim Lovell, Fred Haise, and John "Jack" Swigert agreed to crew *Apollo 13*, they knew it would be risky. But for them, the glories of space travel and being part of NASA's third moon landing outweighed any dangers. They, like most Americans, assumed updates about Apollo 13 would make interesting additions to Cronkite's nightly telecast. But no one could have predicted just how captivating their story would be.

The fire in the *Apollo 1* command module took the
lives of three astronauts.

LIFTOFF

Apollo 13 sits atop the massive Saturn V rocket
that will carry it out of Earth's atmosphere.

Marilyn Lovell

Marilyn Lovell stepped into the shower. She had about an hour to freshen up before joining a handful of other astronaut wives for dinner. Her husband, Jim, was launching into space tomorrow. The day before a launch was always nerve-wracking for her. She hoped her evening plans would keep her distracted.

The 39-year-old housewife was in a foul mood. She was a superstitious person to begin with, so learning that Jim would be on Apollo 13 had worried her. It was such an unlucky number for a space mission. Then, as if to flaunt the number, NASA had scheduled the launch for tomorrow at 13:13 (military time for 1:13 p.m.). She couldn't help but grimace when she thought about it.

Suddenly, a clinking sound startled Marilyn. She looked down and saw her engagement ring fall down the shower drain. She screamed and dropped to her knees. Water streamed into her face. She desperately clawed at the drain but couldn't reach the ring. *Oh no,* she thought. *What a terrible omen.*

Jim Lovell

Cape Canaveral, Florida, April 11, 1970
7:00 a.m.

Jim Lovell squinted into the sunlight. The 42-year-old astronaut stood on a platform suspended 330 feet above Launch Pad A. Lovell glanced down to take in the familiar sights of Florida's Kennedy Space Center. He knew the sprawling facility well. Apollo 13 would be his fourth mission into outer space, and his second trip to the moon. This mission would challenge his crew to land on a mountainous region of the moon. Then they'd explore the moon and do scientific experiments there. It would be a fact-finding mission and a great adventure as well.

Lovell noticed that one of the NASA technicians on the platform looked nervous. He chuckled as he nodded to the anxious tech. This business certainly wasn't for the faint of heart. On one side of the platform was a tiny, cramped elevator and on the other was a towering Saturn V rocket. The rocket, one of NASA's most amazing achievements, housed about 5.5 million pounds of explosive materials. This gigantic bomb was carefully designed to launch three NASA astronauts away from Earth and toward the moon.

Lovell was the commander of Apollo 13. His crewmates soon joined him on the platform. Awkwardly moving in their bulky spacesuits, Fred Haise and Jack Swigert caught Lovell's eye and grinned. Haise and Swigert were younger than Lovell. Haise was 36 and Swigert was 38 years old. Haise had plenty of flying experience with the Navy and Marines, but this would be his first space mission. Swigert had spent thousands of hours flying powerful jets in the Air Force. But, like Haise, he'd never been to space before. All three men had worked as military test pilots.

Lovell smiled at his two friends and colleagues. He was confident that Swigert and Haise would follow his lead on the mission. After all, he knew more than most about space travel. The three men climbed into their craft clumsily and watched as NASA technicians carefully sealed their door. Starting now, they would be breathing the ship's oxygen, eating the ship's prepackaged food, and drinking the ship's water. *Apollo 13* would be their home and life source for the next 10 days.

Launches were long and tedious ordeals. Crews of engineers checked and double checked the safety of each of the craft's systems. The three men tried unsuccessfully to relax for the several hours it took for each system to be prepped.

Finally, at 13:13, Launch Control crackled into their headset radios with the countdown. "Ten, nine, eight, seven, six, ignition, four, three, two, one, zero, liftoff."

A low, booming rumble filled the cockpit. Lovell felt the ship slowly lurch away from the ground. It wasn't a fast liftoff. The enormous

Saturn V rocket was so heavy that it almost hovered off the ground before beginning to accelerate. As the craft rose higher and higher, it gathered speed. Soon he was pinned to his thin seat by the force of the rocket.

Lovell was an even-tempered pilot. He was hardly ever rattled, and he trusted his crew and craft. All the same, he held his hand over the "abort" button for the duration of the launch. All he had to do was press down, and he and his crew would be ejected from the rocket. Parachutes would burst free to help them float safely to the ground.

Now that launch was underway, Lovell gave the official announcement. "The clock is running," he said into his headset. A clock in Lovell's cockpit ticked 0:01.

Gene Kranz

Houston, Texas, April 11, 1970
1:13 p.m.

Gene Kranz's perch at the back of the Mission Control Center (MCC) allowed him to monitor nearly everything and everyone. He looked around the busy room. Three rows of consoles loaded with instruments, screens, and telephones stretched from wall to wall. Each console was occupied by one or two men who were responsible for a particular component of the mission. The floor was sloped so that the front rows of consoles were a few feet lower than the back. This stadium setup gave Kranz the best possible view a flight director could hope for. As flight director, he was responsible for the overall success of this mission and the safety of the crew.

Kranz crossed his arms over his new, white silk vest. His wife had a tradition of making him a vest for each of his missions as flight director. Each flight director headed one of four teams

Gene Kranz monitors a spaceflight from Mission Control Center.

that worked in shifts in the MCC. Kranz was in charge of White Team, so his vest was white. The other teams were Gold, Maroon, and Black. At first, Kranz's vests had raised eyebrows around the Houston Space Center. After all, the square-jawed former Korean War pilot usually stuck to a fairly traditional wardrobe. Like most of his colleagues at NASA, he wore black dress pants, a white button-down shirt, and a black tie. His neat crew cut completed his conservative look. However, over the years, Kranz's team started to look forward to seeing his new vests. Some even told him they thought of his vests as symbols for the spirit of the team.

A screen at the front of the room showed video of the launch. Enormous clouds of steam billowed around the launch pad as the giant rocket ignited. Kranz allowed himself a tiny smile as the Saturn V slowly heaved into the air.

The mood in the MCC was relaxed. After all, this was NASA's fifth mission to or around the moon. Nine months earlier, they'd beaten the Soviets by landing the first humans on the moon. This mission would present new challenges, but it was nothing they couldn't handle.

Kranz wandered over to stand behind the Capsule Communicator (CAPCOM) console. The man at this desk was responsible for all communications between MCC and the space crew. Kranz listened as CAPCOM reviewed various system checks as the rocket roared into the sky. As the mission approached its fifth minute, CAPCOM reassured the crew:

"You're looking perfect. Over."

Commander Lovell responded with a quick "Roger." Suddenly, Lovell's voice snapped across the radio again: "Inboard."

The room erupted in flurries of movement and discussion. The Saturn V's inboard engine had stopped working. This engine was designed to launch the colossal craft up and out of Earth's atmosphere. If it cut out too early, the rocket could lose its momentum and plummet back to Earth.

"Are the remaining engines go?" Kranz barked to the room. "Do we have enough propellant to get the crew up into orbit?" He urgently needed to know if Lovell would have to hit the abort button and eject from the rocket.

Within a minute, the engineers in MCC determined that the rocket's remaining engines could make up for the loss. CAPCOM relayed this message to the crew: "Jim, Houston. We don't have the story on why the inboard out was early, but the other engines are GO and you are GO."

Kranz let out a sigh and joked, "Well, that was our one crisis, boys." Thus far, each mission had experienced a bug or two. Kranz was almost relieved to have Apollo 13's glitch over and done with so soon.

SIDELINED

The crew of Apollo 13. From left: Jim Lovell, Jack Swigert, and Fred Haise.

Ken Mattingly

Houston, Texas, April 11, 1970
4:32 p.m.

Ken Mattingly was depressed. Just days ago he'd been the Command Module pilot for Apollo 13. Now he was sitting in a lower level Mission Control room, listening to the mission over the radio.

Three days before the mission, NASA's flight surgeons realized that Mattingly had been exposed to German measles. Mattingly had never had the disease before. This meant that he could come down with it in just a few days. The flight surgeons worried about how a sick astronaut might behave in space. After careful deliberation, Mattingly had been pulled from the team. Swigert, who had been on the backup crew, gladly replaced him. Now, out of fears that Mattingly could infect other personnel, he wasn't even allowed in the main Mission Control room.

These thoughts were quickly pushed from Mattingly's mind as he heard CAPCOM begin to guide Swigert through a key maneuver. The pilot needed to rearrange the three components of the *Apollo 13* craft. The 11-foot-tall Command Module, nicknamed the *Odyssey*, currently sat at the top of a stack of three spacecraft components. Below it was the 25-foot-long Service Module. This long cylinder contained the guts of the ship. It housed the oxygen tanks, engine, fuel cells, and other tools necessary to sustain life in space.

Finally, below that was the spidery looking Lunar Module, nicknamed the *Aquarius*. This 23-foot-tall craft was meant to ferry Haise and Lovell to the moon. Later they would fly it back up and reconnect with the Command Module.

The current arrangement of *Odyssey*, Service Module, and *Aquarius* was ideal for launch but not for spaceflight. Mattingly listened to the radio as Swigert expertly rearranged the pieces. Swigert turned *Odyssey* around so that the Service Module hung out behind it. Then Swigert precisely docked the nose end of *Odyssey* into *Aquarius*. A few people in Mission Control broke out in quiet applause, but Mattingly just looked down at the carpet. This could have been him. This *should* have been him.

Apollo 13 was going to be an incredible mission. Earlier Apollo missions had tested lunar orbit and the new Lunar Module. *Apollo 11* had landed in the Sea of Tranquility for the first human moonwalk. *Apollo 12* had accomplished a successful lunar landing on the Ocean of Storms. *Apollo 13* planned to land on the mountainous terrain of Fra Mauro. This would test the capacities of both the lunar lander and also the NASA pilots. Mattingly knew he could safely fly his craft. He hoped Swigert could too.

Poppy Northcutt

Cape Canaveral, Florida, April 11, 1970
6:00 p.m.

Poppy Northcutt tied a scarf around her blonde hair as she walked toward her car. The wind was picking up. Luckily it hadn't been an issue during the launch. Northcutt had flown from Houston down to the Cape to watch *Apollo 13* blast off. She'd worked on Apollo 8, but this was the first time she'd witnessed the results of her calculations in person.

Northcutt was still the only female engineer in any of the Mission Control main rooms. She wasn't in MCC yet, where flight director Gene Kranz was currently supervising every detail of 13's flight. She worked in one of the minor Mission Control rooms.

Northcutt hoped that one day she'd earn a seat in the big room. Her job was to help create the computer programs that came up with the trajectory of the spacecraft. Her work on the project had been stellar. She knew she could keep it up.

The press had come to love Northcutt. She was young, beautiful, and fiercely intelligent. And she held her own in a room full of men. NASA loved her too. They occasionally even had a camera trained on Northcutt's tanned face as she did her work. This footage was then broadcast around NASA so other engineers could see what Northcutt was up to. It was an invasion of privacy, sure, but Northcutt allowed it. She didn't want to rock the boat after making it this far.

Life outside NASA was changing. The women's liberation movement had taken hold of pockets of the American population. More women were working outside their homes, advocating for their rights, seeking independence from men. Inside NASA, on the other hand, things were still very male-dominated.

After the successful launch, Northcutt had a feeling the rest of the mission would be fairly uneventful. She decided to get back to work.

Katherine Johnson

Hampton, Virginia, April 12, 1970
1:00 p.m.

Katherine Johnson finished the complex equation on her desk and smiled. The 51-year-old black mathematician stood up from her desk and stretched. She had been working all morning on this new calculation and her back had grown stiff.

Katherine Johnson works on a mathematical equation.

Johnson was a member of the Flight Research Division at NASA's Langley Research Center. Her job was to do the math necessary to devise some of the trajectories needed for the Apollo lunar missions. The agency used mechanical computers for lots of its math now. But it still needed humans like Johnson to come up with the theories behind the math. Many also wanted humans to confirm that the computer's work was correct. Mechanical computers were still fairly new. They sometimes made errors.

Johnson had helped devise the trajectories for several space missions. She even had a bit of a reputation for doing it well. Just before Astronaut John Glenn launched NASA's first Earth-orbiting mission, he'd asked for her specifically. He knew that a computer had come up with his flight path. He wanted Johnson to double check his trajectory one last time. Glenn, like so many others at NASA, knew Johnson had a knack for numbers.

When she wasn't busy doing the math for upcoming missions, Johnson spent her time thinking of new ideas about space.

She often imagined different scenarios a crew could encounter. Then she developed the math they would need to use. In 1967, for example, she and a colleague had wondered what a crew might do if they lost their computers in space. They knew the crew would need a way to get home. They proposed that astronauts who had lost their computers might still be able to navigate if they could see the stars. They could use their view of the stars to line up their ship. Johnson and her colleague then came up with the math to prove this theory and published it in a paper.

As she prepared to start work on another equation, she wondered what new challenges the Apollo 13 crew might face.

Marilyn Lovell
Timber Cove, Texas, April 12, 1970
4:00 p.m.

Marilyn Lovell sat on the edge of the pool and lazily kicked her feet in the cool water. Her neighborhood had been forged by NASA families.

People here were proud of that. So proud, in fact, that the community pool was shaped like a Mercury space capsule.

It was only April, but a hot Texas summer wasn't far off. Marilyn was glad to spend the afternoon by the pool with three of her four children. Her son Jay was away at military school. Marilyn smiled and listened as her daughters, Susan and Barbara, sang bits of popular Beatles tunes. The band had broken up the day before Jim's launch. Barbara had been a mess about it. Marilyn was glad to see the girls smiling again.

Jeffrey, Marilyn's four-year-old, stayed close to her side. She knew he was feeling nervous about his dad's absence. Marilyn couldn't blame him. Spaceflight was still such a new and dangerous endeavor. But all the same, she wanted to reassure her young son.

"Daddy's mission is going just fine," she reminded him.

Jeffrey's smile faded. "I'm still feeling worried," he said quietly.

Marilyn gave a long sigh and slid her sunglasses down onto her face. "Well, baby. That's what the squawk box is for. That noisy little radio is just for us. Daddy's boss at NASA told me we can turn it on and listen to Daddy and his crew anytime we feel worried. We won't be able to talk back to him, but we'll be able to know that he's safe and sound the whole time he's gone."

Jeffrey laid his head on Marilyn's shoulder. She gave him a quick kiss and said, "Honey, everything will be just fine."

Jim Lovell

Command Module cockpit, April 13, 1970
11:30 a.m.

Jim Lovell peered out the tiny window at the black expanse of space. He yawned.

Lovell never really talked about how boring spaceflight could be. Sure, feeling the power of the rockets during launch was exciting. And any time he did a burn — NASA slang for firing an engine — his heart started pumping.

But in between the space maneuvers, space was pretty dull. Floating around was novel at first. But most astronauts could tell you that spending too much time doing flips or spins might give you a queasy belly. And who could forget the time astronaut Bill Anders had lost his lunch all over the interior — and crew — on *Apollo 8*? Lovell shook his head just thinking about that part of his last mission. It was best to stay relatively still and do your work. Lovell wasn't interested in chasing around floating blobs of vomit again any time soon.

Nearly two full days into the mission, Apollo 13 was shaping up to be a success. The only glitches so far were the faulty inboard engine and an oxygen tank that seemed to be giving erratic readings. This was a huge relief.

CAPCOM crackled into their headsets. "The spacecraft is in real good shape as far as we're concerned. We're bored to tears down here."

Lovell chuckled. If the crew down in Mission Control was bored, that was a good sign. He and his crew were safe.

Marilyn Lovell

Marilyn Lovell hurried her two daughters into NASA's private screening room. She didn't want to miss anything. She had listened to her husband's voice over the squawk box at home but she was eager to see his face. Plus, NASA's earlier telecasts had been awe-inspiring programs. They had captured the imagination of the world. She hoped that her husband's broadcast might do the same.

When Marilyn settled in to watch Jim go on the air, a NASA official sat down next to her. "Marilyn," he whispered, "no one is picking up the broadcast. No networks. Nobody."

She looked around and saw that he was right. The screens mounted in Mission Control showed a baseball game, a sitcom, and a talk show.

Marilyn sighed. The country was tired of astronauts. They'd seen the first men go into space and the first moonwalk. Now, too many other events were overshadowing NASA's missions.

29

"We won't tell Jim about the networks just yet," the NASA man told Marilyn. "We'll just let them do the broadcast. Maybe a few stations will pick up a clip for the 10 o'clock news."

Marilyn leaned back and watched as her husband gave a tour of his spacecraft to a nonexistent audience.

Marilyn Lovell discusses the mission with flight surgeon Dr. Charles Berry in NASA's private screening room.

Just before wrapping up the broadcast, a loud clang echoed inside the craft. Jim flinched. The camera panned to Haise, who sheepishly grinned. He was still holding the valve he'd turned. Jim calmly informed the audience, "Every time he does that, our hearts jump into our mouths." Marilyn could tell by her husband's tone that this must be a joke of Haise's. And it sounded to her like the prank was getting old.

After 49 minutes, Jim signed off. "This is the crew of *Apollo 13* wishing everybody there a nice evening. We're just about ready to close out our inspection of *Aquarius* and get back for a pleasant evening in *Odyssey*. Good night."

"HOUSTON, WE'VE HAD A PROBLEM"

3

Gene Kranz

Houston, Texas, April 13, 1970
9:00 p.m.

Gene Kranz poured himself
another cup of coffee and took a sip.
It tasted terrible but at least it was hot.

He absentmindedly listened as CAPCOM guided the crew of *Apollo 13* through a few minor procedures. The ship had to be adjusted constantly. For example, once a day or so, the crew had to do maintenance on their oxygen tanks. Most of the ship's oxygen was kept in supercooled tanks in the Service Module. The temperatures inside were so low that the oxygen resembled a type of frozen slush. Periodically, the crew had to stir the tanks, which meant they had to flip a switch in their cockpit. This switch activated a mechanism in the tanks to both stir and heat up the oxygen slush a little. Stirring the tanks was a way to ensure that oxygen would flow correctly into the spaceship.

There had been a few problems with *Apollo 13*'s oxygen tanks before launch, but it was nothing Kranz was worried about. The mission was going well and the ship was performing just fine. Kranz took another sip of his coffee and grimaced. He tossed it into a nearby trash can. *If NASA can send a man to the moon, they should be able to make a decent cup of coffee,* he thought.

Jim Lovell

Command Module cockpit, April 13, 1970
9:07 p.m.

Jim Lovell listened as CAPCOM finished reading a list of maintenance tasks. Finally, the controller said, "Thirteen, we've got one more item for you. We'd like you to stir up your tanks." Lovell watched as Swigert lazily flipped the switches.

A few seconds later, Lovell heard a loud bang. The ship shuddered and lurched. Instantly, he glared at Haise, who was floating in the tunnel between *Aquarius* and *Odyssey*.

If this was another one of his pranks, Lovell was going to have a serious talk with him. But looking at Haise, Lovell realized he had nothing to do with the commotion. Haise looked terrified.

Lovell spun around as an alarm went off in *Odyssey's* cockpit. Then another. And another. The ship was lighting up with flashing controls and warning buzzers. Multiple systems seemed to be failing. Right in the center of the console, a button marked "Main Bus B" glowed blood red. Lovell's eyes lingered on it. "Main Bus B" was one of the ship's power supplies.

Swigert radioed Mission Control. "I believe we've had a problem here."

CAPCOM responded: "This is Houston. Say again, please."

Lovell jumped in: "Uh, Houston, we've had a problem."

Lovell's mind went to the worst-case scenario. He wondered if a meteoroid had struck *Aquarius*. If it had, the ship could be leaking oxygen.

He quickly sprang toward the tunnel connecting *Aquarius* and *Odyssey*.

He tried to close the hatch between the two to save whatever oxygen remained inside. But something was wrong. He couldn't get the hatch to seal. He frantically pushed and twisted it until he realized that it wasn't going to fit. Finally, he figured that *Aquarius* must not be leaking oxygen. If it had been, they'd all be dead already.

Lovell calmly told Mission Control what his dashboard was telling him. Something had happened to the ship's power supply. It seemed as though *Apollo 13* was in grave danger.

Lovell floated to a window to try to look for any visual signs of damage to the ship. Instead of spotting a faulty panel or switch, he noticed a large cloud of white gas floating into space. He took a deep breath and spoke into his radio: "It looks to me, looking out the, uh, hatch that we are venting something. We are venting something out into the … uh, out into space. It looks like a gas."

Gene Kranz

The Mission Control team burst into frenzied conversations after hearing Lovell speak. What was the gas he had spotted? Why was it leaking?

The Apollo 13 ground crew huddles together in Mission Control as the disaster unfolds.

What was going on with the ship's power? What had happened up there?

In the middle of the chaos, Gene Kranz quietly sat down. He knew what had happened. Of course. How had he missed it?

Kranz felt sure that something, likely an explosion, had damaged one of the ship's oxygen tanks. That would explain what Lovell had seen leaking out into space. And it would also explain the loss of power. The oxygen tanks were located in the Service Module, next to the power supply. If a tank had exploded, it would have damaged the ship's power source.

If he was right, *Apollo 13* wasn't just losing power. It was also losing oxygen.

Kranz stood up. In a calm voice, he announced his theory. Somehow, the mood inside Mission Control became even more frantic. Kranz didn't like it. When people panicked, they made mistakes. He stomped up to the highest level of the room and shouted: "Okay now let's everybody keep cool. Let's solve the problem, team. Let's not make it any worse by guessing."

Lovell wasn't panicked. He had worked as a test pilot for too long to get easily spooked. He was mostly just curious. What was going on with his ship?

Since the original bang and electrical alarms, the ship had begun lurching around in space. He assumed something was wrong with the ship's autopilot. This was a system that normally fired small thrusters to keep the craft on course. Lovell had switched the ship to manual control to see if he could smooth out the ride on his own. This hadn't worked. All his controls felt off. It was like he was flying for the very first time.

While he struggled to steer the craft, he glanced at his oxygen pressure gauges. These told him how much oxygen the ship had. NASA engineers always budgeted for extra oxygen to be safe, so he was shocked at what he saw.

Oxygen tank 2 was reading empty. Oxygen tank 1 was falling. They were in serious trouble.

Lovell looked at the gauges showing how much power the ship had. Two of the three fuel cells were falling and the third was empty.

Mission Control scrambled to walk the crew through various procedures to try to fix the problems. Finally, about 90 minutes after the commotion began, Kranz alerted the crew: "You'd better start thinking about getting into the LM."

Lovell knew that in very dire circumstances, *Aquarius* could be used as a "lifeboat." It had a small amount of oxygen and was a safe vehicle for space orbit. However, he also knew it was meant to support two men for two days. There were three men up here and they needed much longer than two days to get home. He frowned. This could be bad.

Nassau Bay, Texas, April 13, 1970
10:45 p.m.

Poppy Northcutt had left the launch utterly unworried about the safety of the crew. In fact, she'd taken her time on her way back to Mission Control. She'd even stopped at her apartment to unpack and freshen up. As she unzipped her overnight bag, her telephone rang. She answered and was startled to hear the familiar voice of ABC newscaster Jules Bergman.

"Miss Northcutt," Bergman began. "What are the crew's chances of survival? Can you give us any numbers? Are you willing to comment on the disaster?"

Northcutt was stunned. Her mouth hung open in silence. As soon as she realized that *Apollo 13* was in trouble, she snapped into action. She dropped the phone and darted to get her shoes and purse. She needed to get back to Mission Control.

As she grasped the doorknob, she could hear the faint, tinny voice of the famous newscaster calling for her. "Hello? Poppy? *Poppy?*" In her rush to leave, she hadn't set the phone back on the receiver.

She didn't turn back to hang up the phone. There was no time. She slammed the door behind her and ran to her car.

Ken Mattingly

Houston, Texas, April 13, 1970
10:50 p.m.

They had to get out of the *Odyssey*. Now. Ken Mattingly anxiously paced the lower level Mission Control room. The *Apollo 13* crew was currently in the *Odyssey*, but they couldn't stay. Every minute they spent in the fully powered *Odyssey* was draining its precious oxygen and fuel supplies. The crew was going to need the *Odyssey* for the dangerous reentry through Earth's atmosphere. If they used up all its power and oxygen now, it would be useless by that point. And if it was useless, they were dead.

This cone-shaped space capsule was sturdy and relatively roomy. It provided the astronauts with ample protection from the harsh conditions of space. And, it was built with a heat shield. This enabled it to survive the blazing journey through Earth's atmosphere. In other words, it was the only part of the craft that was capable of bringing the crew home.

The view from inside the cockpit of an Apollo lunar module.

Mattingly had spent the last hour listening to murmured conversations around the lower level Mission Control room. It sounded like the crew needed to completely shut down the *Odyssey*. This would save whatever tiny amount of battery power it had left. The crew would need to leave the *Odyssey* powered down until the very last minute. Then they would power it back up for the ride back through Earth's atmosphere.

From what Mattingly could tell, the crew needed to get moving. If they didn't power the *Odyssey* down soon, the ship would drain itself of power completely. This would mean that the astronauts wouldn't be able to turn it back on at all. And if it didn't turn back on at the right moment, they would die.

In addition, the crew also needed to rush to get *Aquarius* powered up. It had a small battery and its own small oxygen supply. It wasn't enough to support three men for the several days they had left of spaceflight. But it was a good place to go while the team figured out what the next steps were.

Mattingly listened to the radio as Mission Control gave the crew the official command. Lovell and Haise exploded into action, turning *Aquarius* on while Swigert turned *Odyssey* off. Typically, this procedure was complex and time consuming. The astronauts didn't have much time. They had mere minutes. They had to work as fast as they could, but still be careful not to make any mistakes. The oxygen supply to the *Odyssey* was almost gone.

Mattingly had heard Gene Kranz talk about moments like this. He'd spoken of times a pilot and crew had to work together in perfect unison and under extreme stress. Kranz called it "looking into the eye of the tiger." *Well*, Mattingly thought, Apollo 13 *is eye-to-eye with that beast right now.*

With mere moments to spare, the crew completed the power-down of *Odyssey* and power-up of *Aquarius*. Mattingly rubbed his eyes. For the moment, the crew was safe.

DECISION TIME

4

A photo of Earth taken by the *Apollo 13* astronauts.

It was shift change time. NASA required its Mission Control workers to take shifts to ensure that people didn't get too tired. Under normal circumstances, Kranz and the White Team would sign off to the Black Team for their shift. But right now nothing was normal.

Kranz wasn't ready to leave. He desperately needed to solve three problems. First, he needed to know how to get his crew home. Second, he needed to figure out how to reduce the amount of power *Aquarius* was using. If he didn't, the power might run out before the crew returned home. Finally, he needed a plan for how to get enough air and water to the three astronauts.

Kranz lobbed these questions to the men at each of his consoles, asking if they had plans or answers. He grimaced as each answered him with a "negative."

One item needed to be decided immediately: How to get *Apollo 13* back to Earth. Right now, the spacecraft was nearing the moon. Soon the moon's gravity would start to pull on it and increase its speed.

Kranz knew he had two options for getting his men home. He could order a direct abort. This involved turning the craft so that its engines pointed toward the moon. The astronauts would then fire the big engines housed in the Service Module to shoot the craft back toward Earth. This would be the fastest way to get *Apollo 13* home, but also the riskiest. It required a big, powerful burn. Under normal circumstances, the spacecraft could handle it. But Kranz worried that the Service Module had sustained serious damage that they didn't know about. This meant that the engine might not work at all, or it could explode and blow up the whole ship.

The second option would be to order a free-return. This meant allowing the craft to continue to approach the moon. When it got close enough, the moon's gravity would pull the ship into orbit. This force would whip the spacecraft around behind the moon. After rounding the moon, the crew would do a small burn with the LM's engines to exit the moon's orbit. If all went well this would fling the craft back toward Earth. A free-return would take much longer than a direct abort, but it would save the crew from testing out the service module's big engine.

Kranz huddled with a few other experts and made his decision. *Apollo 13* would do a free-return. But to speed things up, they'd do a quick burn toward the moon. This would also help tell Mission Control what kind of shape the engines were in.

Kranz ordered MCC to prepare for the burn. The astronauts had to accelerate. But they had to do it in just the right way. Kranz warned everyone, "If this maneuver isn't executed perfectly, you're gonna impact the moon."

"Sorry, Freddo," Jim Lovell said. He had bumped into Haise for the second or third time in as many minutes. The three astronauts had been in the Lunar Module for about two hours, and they were already tired of the cramped space. It was designed to be a tight fit for two astronauts. With three, it was ridiculously tight.

The temperature was also plummeting. In the middle of the chaotic transfer from *Odyssey* to *Aquarius*, Lovell had noticed that a thermometer read 58 degrees. Now it was much colder.

The falling temperatures combined with the three warm bodies crammed inside led to another issue: the windows were fogging up.

"Freddo, could you wipe those windows again?" Lovell asked. CAPCOM had just alerted the crew that they'd be doing a burn to prepare for a free-return course to Earth.

Lovell was a little worried. In order to do a burn, first they needed to point the spacecraft in the right direction. Right now, they couldn't see out the windows to know which way they were pointed.

"It's not going to be easy flying this thing if we can't even see through the glass," Lovell muttered.

Haise used his sleeve to wipe the window. Lovell groaned. He still couldn't see anything. The earlier explosion had produced a cloud of dust and debris. Now it was floating alongside the ship. The cloudy oxygen was also still surrounding them. All Lovell could see when he looked out the window was a mix of sparkling trash and gas.

Lovell wanted to get a glimpse of a star, the moon, or even the sun. A view of one of them could be used to align his engine to face the spaceship the right way. The ship's computers should be able to line him up correctly, but Lovell wanted visual confirmation. They had rushed to power down the *Odyssey* and turn on *Aquarius*. So it was possible that the computer navigation hadn't been set up properly.

If *Apollo 13* wasn't oriented perfectly, a burn could shoot them in the wrong direction. This might send them drifting out into space. Without a reliable engine to get them back on track, this could be fatal.

Poppy Northcutt

Houston, Texas, April 14, 1970
2:00 a.m.

Poppy Northcutt leaned forward at her desk. She listened to the radio as Lovell struggled to get a clear view out the window. She was worried. The computer navigation program she had helped create worked well, but only if it was set up correctly. What if it wasn't?

Northcutt knew that this burn was important. It would alter both the speed of the ship and its course. Right now, the ship was heading toward the moon's orbit, but it wasn't quite where it should be. If it continued on its current course, it would miss Earth by about 40,000 miles.

She calculated a tiny direction change that the ship could take now. She and her team would have the astronauts tweak their orientation by just a fraction of a degree. They would also have it speed up by just 16 feet per second. They were already traveling at about 4,400 feet per second.

These tiny changes might seem insignificant but Northcutt knew that over the course of hundreds of thousands of miles, they would become very important.

Poppy Northcutt reviews mathematical equations with a colleague in one of the Mission Control rooms at NASA.

If everything went well, their work would put *Apollo 13* right where it needed to be for reentry. Northcutt closed her eyes and took a deep breath. The tension was hard to bear.

Ken Mattingly

Houston, Texas, April 14, 1970
2:43 a.m.

Ken Mattingly grasped the yellow controller inside the space capsule and jerked it hard to the right. He watched as a display of stars shifted outside his window. Not enough thrust. He needed more. He flipped a few switches, then tried it again. The stars outside his window shifted again, but he knew it still wasn't enough.

Mattingly was out of time. He climbed out of the replica spacecraft and shook his head to a technician. He and two other astronauts had been in one of NASA's fixed base simulators for an hour. They tried out everything they could think of for Lovell to attempt in his real spacecraft.

Lovell needed to get his ship clear of the debris, but he couldn't waste too much power trying different things. Mattingly and others on the ground tried to help him by simulating different moves on the ground. Nothing had worked.

Mattingly knew how important it was for Lovell to catch a clear glimpse out of his window. Astronauts were trained to use stars as navigational tools. A woman named Katherine Johnson over at NASA's Langley Research Center had even written a paper about it. Mattingly remembered reading it about a year ago. Johnson wrote that even if a ship lost its computers, the crew could navigate home using the stars for reference.

The crew on board *Apollo 13* hadn't lost its computers, but nobody really trusted them right now. They wanted that visual confirmation from a star or two that the ship was properly aligned. It didn't seem like that was going to happen, though. Mattingly sighed. Lovell would have to give up on the idea of seeing where he was going.

Instead, he'd just punch a series of coordinates into his spacecraft's computer and hope for the best.

Mattingly leaned against the outside of the simulator. He listened nervously to the radio transmitting the astronauts as they prepared for the burn. His heart beat wildly as CAPCOM alerted the crew: "You're go for the burn."

The radio crackled. Mattingly imagined what must be happening inside the ship. He knew that the computers would rotate the ship first. After that the engine would kick in — slowly at first and then building in strength. The ship would dart forward for only a few seconds in a small burn.

Less than a minute later, CAPCOM told Lovell to shut down the engine. Lovell did. Now it was done. The question was, had the ship traveled in the right direction? Or was the crew floating off to their deaths?

Just then, CAPCOM spoke. Mattingly could hear the controller's smile through the radio. "No trim required."

Mattingly whooped! Trim was the term used to describe adjustments. If *Aquarius* didn't require any trim, that meant it was on track. The computer's guidance system had worked. *Apollo 13* was still in the game.

Ken Mattingly (left) works with a teammate in Mission Control to help bring the crew home.

LIGHTS OUT

5

The challenges posed by the Apollo 13 mission put the
Mission Control teams to the test like never before.

Gene Kranz

Houston, Texas, April 14, 1970
3:00 a.m.

Kranz stood at the front of a large, windowless meeting room below MCC. After the White Team's shift had ended upstairs, Kranz had directed them all here.

"Alright, men," Kranz began. "From now on the White Team is off-line." He explained that the White Team wouldn't take any more shifts in MCC. Instead, they'd be down here, crunching data to figure out exactly what had happened up there. And more importantly, they were going to figure out how to get their astronauts home.

He noticed how worried some of the faces looked.

Kranz continued, "The odds are darned long, but we're darned good."

He divided them into teams. One would figure out how to get *Odyssey* powered up for reentry. One would work on the ship's trajectory and determine what, if any, burns would be necessary. And one would figure out how to stretch the precious oxygen, water, and power through the rest of the mission.

"If you get tired, we've got people setting up bunks outside." Kranz cracked a smile. "We're calling it 'boy's town,' from what I've heard. But just remember. When you leave this room, you must believe that *this crew is coming home*. I don't care about the odds and I don't care that we've never done anything like this before. Flight control will *never* lose an American in space. Now let's get going."

Marilyn Lovell
Timber Cove, Texas, April 14, 1970
7:00 a.m.

Marilyn Lovell's house was packed. Friends, neighbors, and NASA bigwigs were everywhere she looked. For the most part, it was all fine.

Marilyn was happy for the company and commotion. Neighbors helped with her kids. Friends cooked dinner and kept an endless pot of coffee hot. Her fellow astronaut wives in the house knew exactly what she needed.

Marilyn Lovell anxiously watched the evening news reports covering the Apollo 13 crisis.

They understood the stress and fear she was experiencing. Some people even said they had formed an "Astronaut Wives Club." Marilyn didn't know about that nonsense, but she did know she was grateful for their help.

Marilyn glanced at the door. Father Raise should be here at any moment. She had always been a religious person, but she felt extra comfort in her faith during Jim's missions. Just then, she heard a soft rap at the door. It slowly opened and she spotted the familiar face of their local priest. Father Raise started to smile but his mouth dropped open as Marilyn's daughter Susan shrieked. The young girl sprinted up the stairs sobbing loudly. Marilyn darted up after her, casting a quick wave to the startled priest.

She'd completely forgotten to tell the kids that he would be coming. Susan must have thought that Jim had died!

Gene Kranz

Gene Kranz looked at the men in the room. They were unshaven. Their typically pristine white dress shirts were rumpled and stained. His team was exhausted, but they weren't even close to being done.

Kranz was sitting on a conference room table in his team's makeshift headquarters. He had stopped calling them the White Team at some point, and now they were Tiger Team. He'd been telling them that they were looking into the eye of the tiger, and somehow the nickname had stuck.

Tiger Team had determined that it was going to take about four more days to get the Apollo 13 crew home. Their current dilemma had to do with *Aquarius'* power. In normal circumstances, it needed 55 amps to work. But in order for the power supply to last for four days, they needed to reduce the power usage significantly.

Tiger Team somehow had to get *Aquarius* down to 17 amps. If they couldn't, the ship would run out of battery power and the crew would die.

Jim Lovell

The interior of *Aquarius* was so cold that Jim Lovell could see his breath. It was dark too. Mission Control had them shutting off all kinds of systems, including some of their overhead lights. He knew they needed to cut down on their power usage. He expected more systems would need to be shut down soon.

Lovell crossed his arms over his chest and shivered as he tried to work out what was wrong with the radio. For some reason, their signal was choppy. They were having a terrible time understanding what Mission Control was saying to them. This wasn't just inconvenient.

It was downright scary. They depended on the radio for survival.

Lovell knew that the flight surgeons were worried about the crew's health. They had tasked Fred Haise with taking the first nap. He hadn't been feeling well and the doctors on the ground thought he was most in need of rest. Lovell had asked him a few times if he was okay, but Haise had shrugged and avoided answering. Lovell guessed the poor guy was running a fever.

Jim Lovell tries to sleep inside *Apollo 13*.

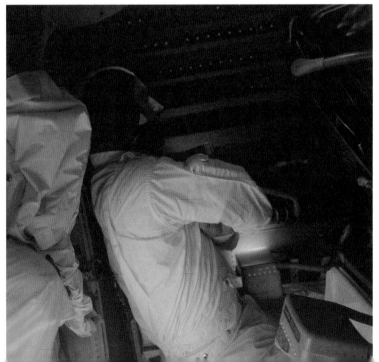

Lovell had watched Haise float up the tunnel to *Odyssey* and strap himself into his sleeping bag. But just a few minutes later, he returned.

"Lovell, nobody's going to get any sleep up there. It's freezing," Haise said, through gritted teeth.

Out of curiosity, Lovell floated into the *Odyssey* to feel for himself. Haise was right. It was probably around 30 degrees up there.

Lovell went back to the radio to try to see if he could get a better signal by adjusting the antennae. Nothing was working. He could barely put together what the crew on the ground was saying. Finally, he pushed away from the controls and turned to Haise. "Freddo, I'm afraid this is going to be the last moon mission in a long time."

Gene Kranz rolled his eyes. He couldn't be upset with Lovell for that "last moon mission" comment, but he sure wasn't happy about it. He knew the crew was exhausted, hungry, and cold. But he also knew that they knew they were constantly being recorded. NASA made all of their communications public. Reporters loved nothing more than to dig up dirt about the goings-on at NASA. The last thing they needed right now was an astronaut who figured the program was toast.

Kranz shook it off. He'd deal with that later.

He had brought his team back into the Mission Control Center to prep the astronauts on their next big maneuver. *Apollo 13* was very close to the moon now. In just 90 minutes, it would orbit behind the moon and lose radio contact.

Kranz wanted to be sure that his team explained the plan to the astronauts before they lost contact. This way, the astronauts could prep and run through the plan while they were behind the moon.

Mission Control was a mess. Sandwich wrappers and half-empty cups of coffee were everywhere. The air was hazy with cigarette smoke.

Kranz listened intently as CAPCOM briefed the crew. After the astronauts rounded the moon, *Apollo 13* would do a major engine burn with *Aquarius'* engine. Kranz was just too nervous about trying to use the main Service Module engine. If it was damaged in any way, a major burn could cause another explosion. So the crew would use the small engine and fire it for 4.5 minutes. This would speed them up an additional 850 feet per second. It would also tweak their trajectory. If all went well, they would land in the Pacific Ocean on April 17, after 142 hours of flight.

The man sitting at the CAPCOM desk raced through the numbers and alignment information for the crew. Just as CAPCOM finished reading through the details, they lost radio contact. *Apollo 13* was behind the moon.

Despite the crisis, the Apollo 13 crew managed to take spectacular photos of the moon.

BURN TIME

A view of the moon from the window of *Aquarius*.

6

Jim Lovell

Aquarius cockpit, April 14, 1970
6:15 p.m.

    The radio was finally quiet. Jim Lovell took off his headset and attached it to the wall with a strap. *Apollo 13* was traveling behind the moon.

This meant that the moon would block any radio signals until they came around to the other side. So, for 25 minutes, their craft would quietly rush through the dark, cold, and quiet of space.

Lovell looked out the window just in time to see the sun set behind the moon. It was called a lunar sunset, and it was spectacular. As the last rays of the sun disappeared behind the moon, the cockpit was plunged into darkness. Lovell was suddenly aware of brilliant stars all around them.

The crew fell silent. Just 139 miles below their tiny windows was the dark side of the moon. Because this side of the moon always faced away from Earth, it had only ever been seen by a few other astronauts. Lovell backed away from the window and let Haise and Swigert snap a few photos.

As light began to shine into the craft once again, Lovell put his headset back on. "Good morning, Houston. How do you read?" he asked.

"Reading you fairly well," CAPCOM said.

It was now time to start prepping for their big burn. Lovell hastily began his checklist, floating from instrument panel to instrument panel. He was nervous and ready to get this underway. He bumped into Swigert on his way to a wall switch. Then as he returned, he had to carefully float behind Haise, who was still taking photos out the window.

Finally, Lovell snapped: "Gentlemen! What are your intentions?" Swigert and Haise looked up, surprised. Lovell continued: "We have a big burn coming up. Is it your intention to participate in it?"

"Jim, this is our last chance to get these shots," Haise responded, sheepishly. "We've come all the way out here — don't you think they're going to want us to bring back some pictures?"

Lovell looked at the camera with a grim smile. "If we don't get home, you'll never get them developed. Now, lookit. Let's get the cameras squared away, and let's get all set to burn."

Poppy Northcutt

Poppy Northcutt could hardly take the suspense. The Apollo 13 crew was in the middle of executing the 4.5-minute burn. If anything went wrong, the mission was toast. And so was the crew. Northcutt listened to the radio as Lovell and CAPCOM exchanged terse updates during the burn. Right now, the crew was accelerating away from the moon and, with luck, headed toward the right spot on Earth.

And then, just as suddenly as it had started, it was over. CAPCOM crackled to Lovell: "That was a good burn."

Lovell couldn't hear him. "Say again?" he asked.

CAPCOM shouted this time: "I SAY THAT WAS A GOOD BURN."

All around Northcutt, people erupted into cheers and hoots. Some came over and patted her on the back.

Northcutt knew they weren't out of trouble yet. The ship was now on the correct course to get home. But they still had to tackle the issue of the rapidly draining batteries. The crew now needed to do an extreme power-down. They needed essentially to shut off everything that wasn't keeping them alive. They'd leave on the communication system, the fan that circulated oxygen, and the water-cooling pumps. Everything else would go dark. Northcutt knew that this had never been attempted in space before. She hoped the crew would be okay.

Jim Lovell

Odyssey, April 15, 1970
3:00 a.m.

Jim Lovell tucked his arms inside his sleeping bag and closed his eyes. Maybe, just maybe, he could catch a few minutes of sleep. He hadn't gotten much shut-eye since the explosion two days earlier.

He figured he might have slept a handful of hours in total since the disaster began. But even as tired as he was, he knew this nap wasn't going to happen. It was so cold he could see his breath collecting around him in a white fog.

Lovell could hear Haise and Swigert clanging around in the *Aquarius* as they powered it down. MCC had them turning off every dial, switch, and gizmo possible. They needed to use less than half of the power the ship normally used. If it wasn't absolutely essential to their survival, it was getting turned off. Lovell knew that his uncomfortable ship was about to get even worse. But if it meant he'd get home alive, he was willing to be cold and hungry for a while.

Haise was talking on the radio. He was saying something about the ship's CO_2 readings. Lovell sighed and pulled himself out of the sleeping bag. This nap was over.

He floated to *Aquarius* to see what Haise was talking about. Carbon dioxide (CO_2) was a toxic gas that the crew naturally created by breathing.

Normally, the levels of CO_2 in the ship remained low. Special filters cleaned the CO_2 out of the air and made it breathable. A typical reading on the CO_2 gauge was usually around 2 or 3. If the filter needed to be changed, it might be 4 or 5. Lovell gasped when he saw the gauge now. It showed a CO_2 level of 13. Lovell stared at the number for a few seconds and then grimaced. Of course. The filters were overloaded. After all, the LM was designed for two men. There were three sets of lungs in here.

Lovell knew that if the gauge levels climbed to 15, the crew would start to suffer from CO_2 poisoning. They could become nauseated, disoriented, and lightheaded. Eventually, they would pass out.

Quickly, Lovell looked for a new CO_2 filter in *Aquarius*. When he didn't see any, he floated over to *Odyssey*. He opened a hatch containing the filters and groaned when he saw them. They were square. The filters in *Aquarius* were cylinders. How on earth was he going to fit a square box into a round hole?

Gene Kranz

Houston, Texas, April 15, 1970
3:38 a.m.

Gene Kranz could hardly believe what he was hearing. CAPCOM was putting his crew through a scavenger hunt in their crippled spaceship. They asked the astronauts to find long underwear, duct tape, plastic wrap, and a slew of other items.

How has the mission come to this? Kranz wondered, shaking his head.

Scientists on the ground had figured out a way to jury-rig the *Odyssey* filter so that it would work in *Aquarius*. Now they just had to teach the astronauts to re-create their makeshift filter using spare items found within *Apollo 13*. This wasn't easy. The ground crew had to describe each step of their process.

CAPCOM began by asking the astronauts to assemble their tools. "You'll need some tape. Give yourself three feet."

"Three feet?" Lovell responded, unsure.

Kranz realized the crew didn't have a measuring tape.

CAPCOM improvised a new instruction: "Make it an arm's length."

For a space crew used to precise, measured, and exact terms, this was utterly unfamiliar. Eventually, after 90 minutes, the crew had done it. Their tape, paper, hose, and plastic creation was ready to plug into the hole for the *Aquarius* CO_2 filter. Swigert proudly proclaimed, "Okay! Our do-it-yourself lithium hydroxide canister is complete!"

A few men in MCC chuckled. It was amazing that Swigert was still cracking jokes up there.

Kranz nodded to CAPCOM, who responded: "Roger. See if air is flowing through it."

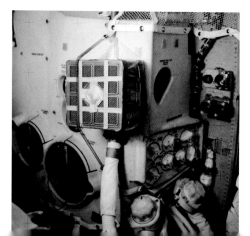

The makeshift air filter constructed out of spare parts, shown here fitted into *Aquarius*.

Kranz jogged over to the console with the CO_2 readings. A crowd had already formed behind the desk. The CO_2 needle began to drop, slowly at first and then with more speed.

A whistle escaped Kranz's teeth. "Okay, that's done." He quietly sighed. Now it was time to start in on the next problem.

Tiger Team needed to find a way to restart *Odyssey* using the small amount of remaining battery power. Typically, powering it up used an order of operations that took multiple days and large amounts of energy. As far as Kranz could tell, they only had about two hours of battery life left in the *Odyssey*. This meant they needed to decide which pieces of equipment were absolutely essential for a safe reentry. Once they came up with that list, they had to figure out the order in which to turn on each item. If Tiger Team made any mistakes down here, the crew could run out of battery power. If they ran out before they made it through Earth's atmosphere, they were dead.

Kranz rubbed his eyes. He wondered if he should try to get some rest.

POWER UP

Jim Lovell in the *Aquarius* cockpit.

Jim Lovell was thinking about coffee. Hot coffee. With a little cream and sugar. He could almost taste it.

Lovell was parched. The crew had been purposefully limiting their water intake to just 6 ounces a day. This was hardly sustainable, but they couldn't risk running out of water. Plus, anytime they did drink water, they created another issue for the ship. In a normal space mission, astronauts urinated into bags. These were then emptied out into space through a venting system. The Apollo 13 crew could no longer vent anything out of fear that it would send their ship off course. Even a tiny spray of liquid could alter the angle of the ship's flight. So, they had to store all of their urine bags. They duct-taped them to the walls of the ship. *The fewer urine bags, the better,* Lovell thought.

Thirst wasn't the only problem. The crew was hungry too. The temperature inside the ship was so low that their food had frozen solid. Earlier that morning, Haise had asked Swigert for a hot dog. Swigert threw over a rock-solid frank. They had been able to laugh only when Haise used it like a drumstick against the wall of the ship.

Now, Lovell looked over at Haise. He didn't seem to be in a joking mood anymore. Lovell could tell he was feeling sick. He looked pale. Lovell guessed he was still running a fever. They were close to finishing this mission, but they still had work to do. He hoped Haise was up to the task.

Just then, CAPCOM crackled onto their radios. It was almost time to start powering up the *Odyssey* for reentry. CAPCOM reminded Lovell and the crew to bring up anything they wanted to keep from the LM into the CM. For a few minutes, the crew packed up cameras, notebooks, and personal belongings and ferried them over to the CM.

Now they prepared to turn *Odyssey* back on. Soon they noticed a familiar problem. The heat from their bodies was warming up the ship. As a result, condensation was forming on the windows, walls, and frighteningly, on the instrument panel. Without gravity, the liquid clung to surfaces. The instruments were supposed to be waterproof but could they withstand this amount of moisture?

"Well," Lovell sighed, "I guess we'll find out soon enough."

Katherine Johnson

Hampton, Virginia, April 16, 1970
1:00 p.m.

Katherine Johnson couldn't concentrate. She kept thinking about that crew up there.

She and her team had spent most of the morning worrying around the coffeepot. They talked and talked about the crew and the disastrous mission. Johnson was the only black woman on her team, but that didn't keep her from having close relationships with her colleagues.

She was brilliant, hardworking, and kind. Her teammates appreciated her in many ways, both personally and professionally.

Johnson glanced quickly at the clock and did yet another mental calculation. The crew had just about 23 hours left until splashdown. She said a quick prayer that their oxygen and power would last.

Ken Mattingly

Mission Control, April 16, 1970
7:30 p.m.

Tiger Team had finally finished its startup list for the *Odyssey*. They had worked, tested, and reworked the list to ensure that the fully powered *Odyssey* would use only 43 amps. If the ship stayed at 43 amps for the rest of the mission, the crew might just survive. If the ship used any more power than that, it could run out of power before it reentered Earth's atmosphere.

Mattingly listened for an hour and forty-five minutes as CAPCOM read item after item. He figured the crew must be scrambling for enough paper to write all this down.

CAPCOM said, "We did run simulations on all of this, so we do think we got all the little surprises ironed out."

Mattingly cracked a smile when Swigert responded, "I hope so, because tomorrow is examination time."

Gene Kranz

Houston, Texas, April 17, 1970
7:00 a.m.

Gene Kranz took a long, deep breath of the cool morning air. He'd stepped out into the parking lot to wake himself up a bit. Looking around, he realized that every parking space was full. There was even a car parked crookedly on the grass near the exit. Kranz felt a swell of pride. His team had dropped everything to be here.

He headed back into MCC to listen as the crew released the Service Module into space. This maneuver wasn't complicated under normal circumstances. Lovell would just need to align his craft and hit a button. But nothing on this mission had been normal. The exhaustion was getting to everyone. Even a simple task could be treacherous if a fatigued commander made a mistake. Plus, nobody knew how damaged the Service Module was. What if the explosion there made it impossible to jettison? The crew couldn't survive reentry with a giant cylinder dragging behind them.

Kranz listened as CAPCOM walked Lovell through the process. Thankfully, the release was uneventful.

Now, Kranz knew, the crew would be glued to their windows. They needed to catch a glimpse of the Service Module as it floated away into space. Kranz hoped they would see something that would give them a clue about what had caused the explosion.

Lovell came onto the radio. "Nothing. Nothing, darn it!"

Kranz closed his eyes in disappointment. Now they would never know what had happened up there. The Service Module would float around in space forever. They'd never have another chance to see it.

Kranz was just standing up to walk away when he heard Lovell's voice.

"There it is! And there's one whole side of that spacecraft missing! Right by the — look out there, would you!" Lovell continued, his voice more excited than it had been during the entire mission. "The whole panel is blown out, almost from the base to the engine," Lovell exclaimed.

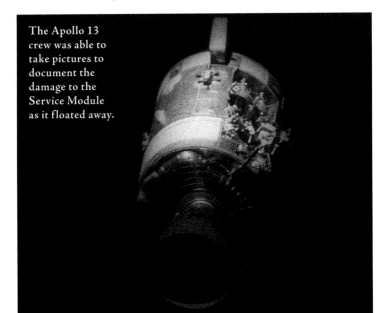

The Apollo 13 crew was able to take pictures to document the damage to the Service Module as it floated away.

Kranz was shocked as he listened to Lovell describe the damage. It sounded like a sixth of the exterior of the Service Module was missing entirely. Tangled shreds of metal and wiring lazily waved in space. Brown burn marks licked the sides of the cylinder. And right where oxygen tank 2 should have been was an empty space.

Lovell was describing a catastrophic issue. It was a miracle the crew had survived at all with that kind of damage.

Kranz elbowed CAPCOM to remind the crew to take as many photos of the damage as possible. For the next 20 minutes, the radio was silent as the three astronauts snapped away.

Finally, Haise's voice crackled onto the radio. "Man," he said, sounding shocked. "That's unbelievable."

CAPCOM came back with a quick joke: "If you can't take better care of a spacecraft than that, we might not give you another one."

For the first time in days, Kranz laughed.

It was time. Jim Lovell was about to turn the cold, dormant *Odyssey* back on. He was worried. No one knew if the ship would power up at all. Or, if it did, they weren't sure how long the power would last. Adding to his worries was the water coating everything. If the ship did manage to power up as planned, the water could cause the electricity to short out.

He glanced at his crew. Haise looked terrible. His fever must have gotten worse. Despite the frigid temperatures in the *Odyssey*, Haise was covered in a fine sweat. Swigert didn't look much better. The sleep deprivation was getting to him. Earlier in the day, Lovell had found Swigert writing a note to himself. The note reminded Swigert not to jettison the Lunar Module while Lovell and Haise were in it. That kind of thing usually didn't require a reminder. Lovell hoped Swigert wouldn't slip up and accidentally send him and Haise out into space.

Lovell took a deep breath and flipped the first switch on his startup list. A tiny light on the dark panel flickered, then glowed green. Lovell hit the next switch and saw another system hum to life. For the next 30 minutes, the three astronauts worked quietly. They flipped switches and pressed buttons. Each time a system came back to life, their shoulders dropped a bit and they felt slightly more relaxed. Finally, they were done. *Odyssey* was operational.

Lovell floated down to *Aquarius* one last time. He was about to jettison it and he wanted to take a few souvenirs. He opened a storage bin and took out the space helmet he would have worn on the moon. It still looked so new. A small, sad smile spread across his face as he tucked the helmet under one arm. He grabbed a few other items, then said goodbye to the Lunar Module. He floated back up to the *Odyssey* and buckled himself into the center seat.

One hundred forty-one hours and thirty minutes into their mission, the crew jettisoned the Lunar Module. It gently floated into space.

CAPCOM crackled into their headsets, quietly saying "Farewell, *Aquarius*, and we thank you."

Lovell and the crew watched as *Aquarius* slowly spun away into space. When it finally became too small to see, Lovell turned back to the control panel in front of him. "Gentlemen," he began quietly. "We're about to reenter."

Haise and Swigert nodded grimly. Each of them knew how risky this reentry was. Their heat shield may have been damaged in the explosion. The ship's wet controls could short out at any moment. Or the ship's batteries could drain, leaving them powerless. This next maneuver would be the most treacherous yet.

Lovell tightened the straps on his harness. "I suggest you get ready for a ride."

The importance of this moment seemed to make each of the astronauts pause. Next to Lovell, Swigert quietly spoke to the crew at Mission Control, "I know all of us here want to thank you guys for the very fine job that you did."

CAPCOM responded with a hint of sadness, "I'll tell you, we all had a good time doing it."

REENTRY

Marilyn Lovell (seated second from right) watches *Apollo 13*'s reentry in her home with friends and family.

Marilyn Lovell

Timber Cove, Texas, April 17, 1970
11:53 a.m.

Marilyn Lovell sat on the floor of her living room, close to the television. The room was still packed with friends, family, and NASA personnel.

At any moment now, her husband would begin the reentry process.

She'd been around for enough space missions to know exactly what was about to happen. Jim's cone-shaped spacecraft needed to punch through Earth's thick atmosphere before it could safely splash down into the ocean. It was speeding around the globe at a precise angle. If it came in too sharply, it would zoom through the atmosphere too quickly, and likely burn up in the process. If the angle was too shallow, the ship would skip right off the atmosphere and be sent hurtling out into space. Marilyn knew that the angle of Jim's spacecraft looked good for reentry. She'd listened to the squawk box all day, piecing together enough information to feel confident. But no one knew if the spacecraft was going to be able to survive the heat and speed of reentry.

Jim would hold the spacecraft in position so that it blasted toward Earth rump-first. When it hit the atmosphere, the ship would start to slow down. The friction this caused would generate heat. Lots of heat. The tiny spacecraft would be wrapped in temperatures of up to 5,000 degrees Fahrenheit. Jim had spoken about the reentry he'd experienced during Apollo 8. He had watched out his window as the air turned orange, and then red, and then as flames surrounded his ship. If there were any cracks or weak spots in the heat shield, Marilyn knew the crew would not survive.

Usually, reentry took about 3 or 4 minutes. The spacecraft would lose radio signal during this time. Marilyn knew well how long those few minutes could feel.

Her squawk box crackled to life. Marilyn had taken to moving it around her house so that it was always nearby. Now she heard CAPCOM radio her husband from the corner of her living room:

"*Odyssey*, Houston. Everyone says you're looking great. We'll have loss of signal in about a minute. Welcome home."

Marilyn closed her eyes and took a deep breath. Her crowded living room fell silent. The tension was almost unbearable.

The squawk box reminded everyone of the ticking time. After about 3 minutes, CAPCOM started trying to raise the crew. "*Odyssey*, Houston. *Odyssey*, Houston. Standing by, over." For a full minute, there was no answer. Marilyn refused to let doubt enter her mind. She just knew it would be okay. Everything would be okay. It had to be.

Finally, a tinny voice jumped out of the squawk box. "Okay, Joe." Marilyn howled with relief. It was Jack Swigert. The crew was okay. Somewhere in the background, she heard a bottle of champagne pop open.

Marilyn's neighbor tapped her on the shoulder. At first, Marilyn hardly noticed the sensation. She was too busy hugging her daughter Barbara, who was crying from relief. Finally, her neighbor announced loudly, "Marilyn, the president is on the phone."

Marilyn looked up, bewildered and overwhelmed. She followed her friend into the kitchen and picked up the telephone.

"Marilyn, this is the president," began the familiar voice of Richard Nixon. He continued, "I wanted to know if you'd care to accompany me to Hawaii to pick up your husband."

Nearly exploding with relief, Marilyn responded: "Mr. President, I'd love to."

Jim Lovell

Above the Pacific Ocean, April 18, 1970
4:00 p.m.

Jim Lovell looked out the airplane window. Below him stretched the crisp blue Pacific Ocean. It was hard to believe he'd safely splashed down there yesterday. He thought about the reentry again. The three astronauts had been strapped into their chairs, feeling the incredible force of the ship slowing down.

Suddenly, it began to rain inside the CM. Or at least it seemed like rain. The water that had collected on the ship's surfaces — the water he'd been so worried about — began falling. It fell off the walls, ceiling, and instruments in droplets. It was as though the astronauts were caught in a downpour.

(From left) Jack Swigert, Jim Lovell, and a U.S. Navy underwater demolition team swimmer wait to board the helicopter that will take them to the *Iwo Jima* rescue ship.

After splashdown, the naval ship *Iwo Jima* had picked them up. Haise had been rushed off to the sick bay immediately. But Lovell and Swigert had showered, shaved, and enjoyed an incredible meal. In fact, Lovell realized as he shifted uncomfortably, he probably should have paced himself a bit more on that dinner. He'd lost 14 pounds during his mission. Eating so much shrimp, lobster, and prime rib all in one sitting had made him feel ill.

He checked his watch. They should be landing in Hawaii in about an hour. He couldn't wait to see Marilyn. He knew this mission must have been terrible for her and the kids.

Fred Haise sat down in an empty seat next to Lovell. He was looking much better. His fever was down, and whatever medication they had given him must have started working. Haise handed Lovell a stack of newspapers and grinned. The paper on top of the stack was *The New York Times*. In giant, black letters, the front page proclaimed: "Astronauts Land Gently on Target, Unharmed by Their Four-Day Ordeal."

Lovell looked at the headline for a moment. Then he smiled at Haise and swiveled around to see Swigert napping a few rows back. *I suppose that headline is accurate,* he thought. *But that sure does leave out a few details.*

While aboard the *Iwo Jima*, Jim Lovell reads a newspaper account of the Apollo 13 mission.

EPILOGUE

Hours after *Apollo 13* splashed down in the Pacific Ocean, NASA launched an investigation into what had gone wrong. This showed that over the many stages of construction, testing, and transportation, the wiring inside oxygen tank 2 became faulty. When Jack Swigert stirred the tanks, a spark inside tank 2 caused an explosion.

(From left) Fred Haise, Jim Lovell, and Jack Swigert, aboard the *Iwo Jima* after splashing down in the Pacific.

The force from that explosion caused irreparable damage to *Apollo 13*.

Apollo 13 taught people many important lessons. One of its most lasting lessons was not related to spaceflight or engineering. Rather, it had to do with teamwork. The final report from the investigation summarized: "Perfection is not only difficult to achieve, but difficult to maintain. The imperfection in *Apollo 13* constituted a near disaster, averted only by outstanding performance on the part of the crew and the ground control team which supported them."

Following their safe return, President Nixon gave each member of the Apollo 13 crew the Presidential Medal of Freedom. Jim Lovell never went into space again. In 1973 he retired from NASA to work in different corporate jobs. He was inducted into the U.S. Astronaut Hall of Fame in 1993. The following year he published a book with coauthor Jeffrey Kluger about his experiences on *Apollo 13*. Today Lovell remains active, traveling to give lectures and talk to audiences about his experiences.

Marilyn Lovell never broke down during Jim's missions. But shortly after Jim's return, she became extremely upset when Jim left for a quick business trip. She couldn't calm herself. NASA had always pressured the astronaut's wives to maintain a perfect public image. This meant that they could never show stress or fear. Seeing a therapist could ruin this image. It would reveal that the wives were struggling with the stresses of being married to astronauts. However, Marilyn knew she needed professional help. She began seeing a psychiatrist who helped her cope with her fears and emotions.

In the years after Jim retired from NASA, Marilyn remained close with other astronaut families. She organized get-togethers and even went on trips with other astronaut families. She later reflected on her time with the other NASA families, saying: "Those were the best years of my life."

Ken Mattingly was grateful to have been on the ground during the Apollo 13 mission. He had a particular health issue that could have proved catastrophic in the ship's freezing temperatures. In an interview, Mattingly said: "When my body gets below 60 degrees, it doesn't function. If I had been stuck up there, I would have absolutely been a disaster."

Mattingly went on to fly *Apollo 16*, and also flew in an orbital test of the space shuttle. He retired from NASA in 1985.

People around the world followed the events of Apollo 13. This postage stamp from the United Arab Emirates commemorates the mission.

APOLLO 13

1.50 RIYALS AIRMAIL EVENTS OF 1970 برید جوی ١,٥٠ FUJEIRA الفجيرة ريالات

Gene Kranz and the rest of his crew received the Presidential Medal of Freedom Team Award. Kranz was incredibly proud of the work he and his team had accomplished. He remained an important person at NASA for years after Apollo 13, working on such projects as the space shuttle. He retired from NASA in 1994, but continued to work in aviation, consulting on airplane designs. In 2000 his memoir about his time at NASA, *Failure Is Not an Option: Mission Control from Mercury to Apollo 13 and Beyond*, was published.

Poppy Northcutt received the Presidential Medal of Freedom Team Award for her work on Apollo 13. Though she did not remain at NASA for long, she left her mark on the community. She even has a lunar landmark, Crater Poppy, named in her honor. In the years following Apollo 13, Northcutt became very active in the women's liberation movement. She became a leading figure in the National Organization for Women (NOW). Northcutt graduated from law school in 1984 and became a respected criminal defense lawyer.

Katherine Johnson's calculations helped the Apollo 13 astronauts perform one final lifesaving course correction before they reentered Earth's atmosphere. She went on to work on many other important space projects, such as the space shuttle. Johnson remained at NASA until retiring in 1986 after 33 years of work. Over the course of her career, she received many awards for her accomplishments in space science. She was also recognized for her role as an African-American trailblazer. In 2015, she received the highest civilian honor: the Presidential Medal of Freedom.

The people of Mission Control celebrated once the crew reached the *Iwo Jima*.

TIMELINE

MAY 25, 1961 President John F. Kennedy gives a speech before Congress announcing that an American will land on the moon and return safely to Earth before the end of the decade

OCTOBER 27, 1961 The first rocket to be used in the Apollo missions, SA-1, is tested for the first time

NOVEMBER 22, 1963 President John F. Kennedy is assassinated in Dallas, Texas

1965 Construction begins on Oxygen tank 2

FEBRUARY 3, 1966 Luna 9, an unmanned Soviet spacecraft, makes the first successful landing on the moon

JUNE 2, 1966 NASA's Surveyor 1 performs the United States' first successful unmanned landing on the moon

JANUARY 27, 1967 *Apollo 1* catches fire during a test on the launch pad, killing all three crew members onboard

OCTOBER 11, 1968 The first manned Apollo mission, Apollo 7, successfully launches. The crew performs an 11-day mission which includes the first live television broadcast of people in space

DECEMBER 21–27, 1968 Jim Lovell orbits the moon on *Apollo 8*. The crew members are the first people to see the side of the moon that faces away from Earth

MARCH–MAY, 1969 Apollo 9 and 10 launch, both conducting important tests of the Lunar Module

JULY 16–23, 1969 Apollo 11 travels to the moon

JULY 20, 1969 Neil Armstrong becomes the first human to walk on the moon

1:13 P.M., APRIL 11, 1970 Apollo 13 lifts off

9:07 P.M., APRIL 13, 1970 Oxygen tank 2 explodes, severely damaging *Apollo 13*

10:50 P.M., APRIL 13, 1970 *Apollo 13* crew moves into *Aquarius*

6:15 P.M., APRIL 14, 1970 *Apollo 13* disappears behind the moon

8:50 P.M., APRIL 14, 1970 *Apollo 13* performs large engine burn to speed up and refine its trajectory

3:38 A.M., APRIL 15, 1970 *Apollo 13* crew creates its own air filter out of spare parts, following instructions from Mission Control

7:14 A.M., APRIL 17, 1970 *Apollo 13* jettisons its Service Module

10:43 A.M., APRIL 17, 1970 *Apollo 13* jettisons *Aquarius*

12:07 P.M., APRIL 17, 1970 *Apollo 13* splashes down in the Pacific Ocean

JANUARY 1971–DECEMBER 1972 *Apollo 14, 15, 16,* and *17* each successfully land on the moon. Humans have not landed on the moon since the *Apollo 17* crew did so in 1972.

JANUARY 5, 1972 President Richard Nixon announces the development of the space shuttle, NASA's reusable launch vehicle

GLOSSARY

amp (AMP)—a unit used to measure the strength of an electrical current

atmosphere (AT-muhss-fihr)—the mixture of gases that surrounds Earth

condensation (kahn-duhn-SAY-shuhn)—water that collects in small droplets on a cold surface

jettison (JET-uh-sehn)—to release or drop something from an aircraft or spacecraft in flight

lunar (LOO-nuhr)—having to do with the moon

meteoroid (MEE-tee-ur-oyd)—piece of rock or other matter traveling through space

orbit (OR-bit)—the path an object follows as it goes around the Sun, the moon, or a planet

trajectory (truh-JEK-tuh-ree)—the path followed by a projectile, such as a spacecraft

CRITICAL THINKING QUESTIONS

1. What were some of the barriers in place for women working at NASA?

2. Jim Lovell ultimately called the mission a "successful failure." What were some of the major ways the ground crew came together to support the space crew? How did these actions make the mission a success

3. How did Gene Kranz unify and motivate his team?

INTERNET SITES

Use FactHound to find Internet sites related to this book.

Visit *www.facthound.com*

Just type in 9781515779407 and go.

FURTHER READING

Adamson, Thomas K. *Apollo 11 Moon Landing: An Interactive Space Exploration Adventure*. North Mankato, Minn.: Capstone Press, 2017.

Feldman, Thea. *Katherine Johnson (You Should Meet)*. New York: Simon Spotlight, 2017.

Morgan, Ben, ed. *Space! The Universe as You've Never Seen It Before*. New York: DK Publishing, 2015.

Reynolds, David. *Apollo: The Epic Journey to the Moon 1963–1972*. Minneapolis: Zenith Press, 2013.

Rissman, Rebecca. *Hidden Women: The African-American Mathematicians of NASA Who Helped America Win the Space Race*. North Mankato, Minn.: Capstone Press, 2018.

SELECTED BIBLIOGRAPHY

Chaikin, Andrew. *A Man on the Moon: The Voyages of the Apollo Astronauts.* New York: Penguin Books, 2007.

Houston, Rick. *Go, Flight! : The Unsung Heroes of Mission Control, 1965–1992.* Lincoln, Nebr.: University of Nebraska Press, 2017.

Koppel, Lily. *Astronaut Wives Club: A True Story.* New York: Grand Central Publishing, 2014.

Kranz, Gene. *Failure Is Not An Option: Mission Control from Mercury to Apollo 13 and Beyond.* New York: Simon & Schuster, 2000.

Lovell, Jim, and Jeffrey Kluger. *Lost Moon: The Perilous Voyage of Apollo 13.* Boston: Houghton Mifflin, 1994.

INDEX

ABOUT THE AUTHOR

Rebecca Rissman is an award-winning children's author. She has written more than 200 books about science, history, art, and culture. Her writing has been praised by *School Library Journal*, *Booklist*, *Creative Child Magazine*, and *Learning Magazine*. She lives in Chicago, Illinois, with her husband and two daughters.